HAWK & DROOL

GROSS STUFF IN YOUR MOUTH

Written by Sandy Donovan

Illustrated by Michael Slack

M Millbrook Press • Minneapolis

To Mara, Jereth, and Triston
-Michael Slack

Millbrook Press
A division of Lerner Publishing Group, Inc.
241 First Avenue North
Minneapolis, MN 55401 U.S.A.

Website address: www.lernerbooks.com

Library of Congress Cataloging-in-Publication Data

Donovan, Sandra, 1967–
    Hawk & Drool : gross stuff in your mouth / by Sandy Donovan ; illustrated by Michael Slack.
     p.   cm. — (Gross body science)
    Includes bibliographical references and index.
    ISBN 978-0-8225-8966-2 (lib. bdg. : alk. paper)
    1. Saliva—Juvenile literature. 2. Mouth—Diseases—Juvenile literature.
  3. Dental plaque—Juvenile literature. I. Slack, Michael H., 1969– ill. II. Title.
III. Title: Hawk and drool.
  QP191.D66 2010
  612.3'13—dc22   2008050699

Manufactured in the United States of America
1 2 3 4 5 6 — BP — 15 14 13 12 11 10

CONTENTS

CHAPTER 1

SLIMY AND SLOPPY

YOUR SALIVA

Sometimes you hawk it up. Other times you drool it out. You might know saliva by its nickname—spit. It's that slimy stuff that helps you hawk, drool, and make spitballs. Or win spitting contests. Not that you know anything about either one of these. Yes, spit has its uses when it comes from your own mouth. But maybe you'd rather not see—or, even worse, touch—other people's spit. It's one of the more disgusting parts of the human body, after all. You may not want to think too much about it, really.

Where does spit come from? Check out this close-up of a gooey, mucus-coated salivary gland. Yuck!

But spit isn't really any nastier than other parts of your body. Spit is made up of ordinary body things: mostly water and chemicals. And it helps you do lots of things besides wet down spitballs. Things you really wouldn't want to live without—eating, for instance.

Take a closer look, and decide for yourself how disgusting spit really is.

WHAT IS THAT SLIMY, SLOPPY STUFF?

Saliva. Spit. Drool. Dribble. Whatever you call it, everyone has it. The inside of your mouth lives in a constant bath of spit—and you can't get rid of it. In fact, you're swallowing saliva all the time. And merely thinking about that probably made you take a swallow just now! You could make a thousand spitballs a day, and you wouldn't run out of saliva. Your body keeps on making it, twenty-four hours a day, seven days a week.

5

Spit is almost entirely water. (Nothing gross about water, right?) But it has a few important ingredients added in. One is mucus—the stuff that makes saliva slimy. MMMM . . . YUMMY. Another is lysozyme, a chemical that kills the germs that grow in your mouth. There's also something called salivary amylase, a chemical that helps break down food.

So where exactly does saliva come from? Ever heard of a saliva factory? Well, you're walking around with one tucked right between your nose and your chin. That's right! Your mouth is your own personal saliva maker.

Inside your mouth are hundreds of salivary glands. Each of these little groups of cells makes and releases saliva into the mouth. Throughout the day, they make more saliva to prepare for eating. Certain thoughts or activities can really spur these glands into action. Ever notice how your mouth starts watering right before you take a bite of something yummy? That's your salivary glands springing into action. You don't even have to take a bite for the effect to work. Try walking past a bakery window loaded with cupcakes, and your glands will probably kick into high gear. Heck, just *thinking* about a bakery window full of cupcakes will probably do the trick. **What gets your saliva flowing?** A double cheeseburger with a side of fries? Or a hot fudge sundae, loaded with extra whipped cream?

Saliva made in the salivary glands really starts dripping when you think of something tasty!

A typical mouth makes enough saliva in one day to fill about six cans of soda, each day, every day. And guess what? You swallow almost all of that spit!

You have hundreds of salivary glands, but most of the action takes place in the following three main pairs:

- **Parotid glands** are found on the upper part of each cheek, near your top molars (back teeth).
- **Submandibular glands** are found on the bottom of the mouth, by the lower front teeth.
- **Sublingual glands** are located right under the tongue.

So when your mouth starts watering, you usually notice it near your back teeth, under your tongue, or right behind your lower front teeth. But up to one thousand more salivary glands—very tiny ones— are scattered throughout your

Saliva made in the glands travels to the mouth through tubes called ducts.

mouth. Among other places, they're inside your lips and cheeks, on the back of your tongue, and at the back of your throat. That's why there's no escaping it anywhere in the mouth. Spit is everywhere.

GROSS FACT #2

With each sneeze, up to one hundred thousand drops of mucusy saliva come spewing out of your mouth. So remember to cover your mouth as well as your nose!

SO WHAT GOOD IS SALIVA?

Thinking about all that gooey saliva you make and swallow might make you squirm. But in fact, it's a good thing you're a walking saliva factory, because your body needs saliva. And not just for hawking, drooling, and making spitballs. (That's right. There's more to life than spitballs.)

Cake becomes goo with a little help from saliva!

For one thing, you wouldn't be able to eat without saliva. Sure, maybe you could drink. And slurp down a bowl of soup or a smoothie. But bread? Chips? A slice of pizza? Forget about it. Before you can swallow any of those foods, you need to change them from a basically dry, solid shape into a mashed-up ball that will both fit and move down your throat.

And guess what is perfectly suited for that job? Yep, this is what saliva was made for. As soon as you take a bite, saliva goes to work. It covers every bit of solid food with a **gross, mucusy coating**. After a little help from your teeth and your tongue, that bite of sandwich, pizza, or chips no longer resembles the food you put in your mouth. Instead, it's a softened-up ball of goop. Then it's on to your stomach, where your body will break it down for energy.

After

Before

But not so fast. Even before saliva moistens your food, it helps you taste. Your body tastes things through thousands of taste buds on your tongue and inner mouth. When food touches taste buds, they send a message to your brain. The message tells your brain whether the food is sweet, salty, sour, or any combination of flavors. But there's a catch: dry taste buds can't sense taste. Enter saliva. By wetting the taste buds, it allows them to do their job.

This may not look very nice, but it's a taste bud. Thousands of these little guys let you taste everything from ice cream to broccoli.

A SWEET EXPERIMENT

Curious about the way saliva turns starch into sugar? Try this simple experiment. Place a chunk of bread on the top of your tongue. The bread probably has very little taste. Then start chewing. The bread will become coated with saliva. Do you begin to notice a sweet taste? That's salivary amylase at work.

Saliva also helps your body get a head start on digesting, or breaking down, food. Besides covering each bite in **sloppy goo**, it actually starts to break it down. Remember salivary amylase? That's the enzyme—or chemical—that begins digestion. It breaks down starches—bread, pasta, cereal, and similar foods like chips. Think about a big glob of half-chewed bread or cereal in your mouth. **Disgusting, right?** That's just salivary amylase at work.

Saliva has one other important function. It's a key soldier in your body's battle against germs. It helps to wash away tiny bits of food—and keep them from sticking to your teeth and mouth. It also has a secret weapon—an ingredient called lysozyme. This chemical actually fights the germs that grow in your mouth. What? You have germs growing in your mouth? That's right! For more details on how your mouth is a breeding ground for germs, check out chapter 2.

GROSS FACT #3

Besides water, mucus, and the chemicals already mentioned, saliva has a few other ingredients. Two of those are urea and uric acid. Sound a lot like urine? Yep, urea and uric acid are waste products most commonly found in urine. *YUCK!*

WHAT'S THAT SMELL?

BAD BREATH

Picture this. You're huddled in a circle with your friends, and someone tells a really funny joke. Everyone starts laughing. But suddenly, one of your friends puts his hand over his nose and shouts, "Ugh! Someone's breath smells like a garbage truck!" Now you start to panic. Is it me? Did I forget to brush? Did I eat a stinky lunch?

Check out these little guys. They're just one example of the bacteria that are right at home inside your mouth.

Worrying about things like bad breath is part of growing up. When you were a little kid, you may not have cared too much about how you smelled. You might have even thought it was funny to gross people out with stinky breath. But now? Ugh! What could be more embarrassing than hearing that your breath smells like a fuzzy, holey pair of worn-out gym socks?

A MOUTH FULL OF GERMS

So what causes that smell that gets your friends to hold their noses and even makes your dog look at you funny? Bacteria! Bacteria are tiny little creatures that live on your teeth, your tongue, and whatever else they find. That's right. Your mouth is teeming with millions of creepy, crawly critters. *EEEWW!*

HOLD THE ONIONS?

Not all stinky breath comes from mouth bacteria. Sometimes stinky food like garlic, hot peppers, or onions will leave you with breath that can clear a room. (Try eating something with all three to brew the world's nastiest breath!) Those foods contain strong-smelling oils that get into your lungs. Then the smell is released every time you breathe out. Yuck! Your poor friends and family! But don't worry. The smell will fade a few hours after your meal. In the meantime, keep the sugar-free gum or mints handy!

But don't worry about your mouth being a huge bacteria hotel. Bacteria are everywhere, including in our bodies. And not all of them are bad. Some bacteria do good things for us, like helping us digest our food. It's the bad bugs you want to watch out for. These bacteria can make us sick and cause infections.

They can also cause bad breath. And if we let them build up in our mouths, they can cause more serious trouble—like tooth decay. YIKES! Kind of makes you want to brush your teeth, doesn't it?

But wait a minute. How do these little creatures even live inside a mouth? Isn't it dark and wet and gross in there? Yep! And that's exactly the environment that bacteria love. Plus, living in a mouth gives them an extra bonus: we are constantly providing them with breakfast, lunch, and dinner. They also get snacks, deserts, sodas, and more. It's no wonder they want to stick around!

GROSS FACT #4

Ugh! You've got halitosis! No, it's not some new and deadly disease. It's just a fancy way of saying bad breath. And the cure is usually simple. Just grab a toothbrush and get to work!

Bacteria feast on the little scraps of food you leave behind after you've swallowed most of your meal. Think about it. Every time you eat a sandwich or piece of pizza, you leave enough leftovers in your mouth to feed an army of bacteria. Once you've swallowed your last bite and moved on from the table, that's when the bacteria get started on their meal. As they chomp away on your leftovers, they produce a stinky chemical called hydrogen sulfur. And when the sulfur escapes out of your mouth, your friends start to tell you that your breath smells like a garbage truck.

This is just one kind of bacteria (purple) that thrives on the food that gets left in your mouth after you eat.

Behold the mighty amoeba! It may not win any beauty contests, but this little critter helps clear out the germs in your mouth.

KEEPING YOUR BREATH STINK FREE

So how do you prevent stinky breath? You can't get rid of all the bacteria in your mouth. And you can't stop eating. Well, not for more than a few hours, anyway. But what you can do is rely on your body's very own secret weapon against mouth bacteria: mouth amoebas! Mouth amoebas may sound like weird creatures from a late-night science fiction film. But they're really one of your body's many defenses against bad germs. These little buglike creatures fight bacteria by eating them alive!

Now, you might be a little freaked out to hear that you have even *more* tiny bugs floating around in your mouth. But mouth amoebas really are helpful. Not only do they munch on all that nasty bacteria. They also gobble up any little extra food scraps they find on your teeth. That leaves bacteria less food to picnic on. And you end up with better-smelling breath!

Check out all the stuff you can clear off your teeth by brushing and flossing!

Mouth amoebas are a cool weapon in the fight against stinky breath. But unfortunately, they can't win the war alone. It's up to you to help out by keeping your mouth as clean as you can. A toothbrush and floss are your own best weapons. I know, I know. Brushing and flossing probably aren't your favorite things to do. But now that you know about the millions of tiny bacteria living in your mouth, you can see how huge of a deal oral hygiene really is. So what are you waiting for? Pull out that toothbrush and get busy!

ROT and DECAY

YOUR TEETH

All those tiny bacteria hanging out inside your mouth can do more than cause stinky breath. If you give them the chance, they'll eat away at your teeth. Yikes!

But wait a minute! How can tiny little creatures bring down something as hard as a tooth? Read on to find out.

A CLOSER LOOK AT YOUR CHOMPERS

Most kids have twenty-eight teeth—fourteen on the top and fourteen on the bottom. Right up front are eight incisors—four on the top and four on the bottom. Incisors are sharp like knives for biting and cutting food. Next come four canines—one on each side, top and bottom. These pointy teeth help tear chunks of food when biting. Next, you have two premolars—and then three molars on each side, top and bottom. Premolars have two pointy peaks, and molars have three pointy peaks. These teeth in the back of you mouth are for chewing and grinding up food so it can be swallowed. Mmm, feeling hungry?

If you want to keep that pearly white smile for the
rest of your life, you need to take good care of your
chompers. And that goes double for those permanent
adult teeth. After all, your permanent teeth need to
last for the rest of your life. There's no tooth fairy
to reward you if you lose your permanent teeth! And
there's no replacement teeth waiting to take over
either. In other words, what you have is what you get.

Whoa! Check out what a set of chompers looks like with an X-ray!

This is a cross section of a healthy tooth. The outer part is the enamel, and the darker part in the middle is the dentin.

Luckily, your teeth are pretty tough. The inside of a tooth is stuffed with dentin. That's a hard yellow goop. Dentin gives teeth the strength to chomp down on food. The dentin is protected by a layer of enamel on the outside. This tough outer layer is the part of the tooth we can see. It's a whitish or yellowish color. (Ugh—yellowish?! Yep! Yellow can be a perfectly natural color for a tooth.)

Inside the dentin is the tooth's pulp. This is a soft, sensitive part that's packed with blood vessels and nerves. Hmm . . . I think I feel a toothache coming on.

GROSS FACT # 6

Some scientists think that naturally yellow teeth may be stronger than naturally white teeth. (Um, no, this doesn't mean you should stop brushing. They're talking about *naturally* yellow teeth.)

25

ATTACK OF THE PLAQUE

Look out! Something's attacking your teeth—right now! That something is plaque. Plaque is a sticky coating that grows on your teeth. What?! A sticky coating is growing on your teeth? That's right. Check it out if you don't believe me. Scrape a fingernail gently along the flat part of one of your front teeth. Take a look under the fingernail. See anything gooey or gross? That's plaque.

It's when you don't brush the plaque away that trouble starts. When plaque stays on teeth for too long, it starts to harden. It takes less than two weeks for it to get pretty much rock solid. The hardened plaque is called tartar. If you're wondering if you have any, take a look behind your lower front teeth. Can't see back there? Try using a small mirror.

Plaque isn't pretty.

ALL ABOUT THE BRUSH

Historians believe the first people to use an object to clean their teeth were the ancient Babylonians in 3500 B.C. They used twigs to scrape food off their teeth. By about 1600 B.C., the Chinese had perfected the twig toothbrush. They chewed one end down until it was soft and slimy—perfect for using as a brush. Then they chewed the other end into a point for doing the heavy scraping. By the A.D. 1800s, tools that resembled modern toothbrushes were being made in Great Britain. The handle was carved from cow bone, while the bristles came from the hair on pigs' necks. And wouldn't you just love to rub pigs' hair all over your teeth?

See any hard white or yellowish stuff stacked up on your teeth right next to your gums? That's tartar. I know what you're thinking: Get it off! Fast! Unfortunately, once plaque hardens into tartar, you won't be able to get it off by brushing. Or flossing. Only someone at a dentist's office can scrape tartar off your teeth.

Plaque looks even worse when you get a super close-up view!

GROSS FACT #7

You might be a plaque and tartar factory. About one in ten kids is! If so, your mouth naturally grows plaque and tartar more quickly than most.

WHEN THINGS GET REALLY ROTTEN

Think having a mouth full of plaque and tartar sounds pretty gross? Actually, the crud is pretty harmless as long as you remember to brush at least twice a day, floss, and see a dentist regularly. The real tooth decay and rot happens when you don't do these things.

When the bacteria in your mouth find bits of food to feast on, they create acid. (Acid is a sour substance that eats away at other things.) Sugar is a favorite food of bacteria. So when you eat a lot of sugar, you're inviting the bacteria to make more acid. Mouth acid eats away at your teeth. Often your saliva neutralizes mouth acid before it can do any harm to your teeth. (This means it mixes with the mouth acid and stops it from eating away at your teeth.) But if the acid is created inside a layer of plaque or tartar, the saliva can't do its job. That's when the acid starts to eat away at your teeth. And that's what gives you a cavity. A cavity is a rotten spot in your tooth.

First, a cavity breaks through the hard enamel surface of the tooth. It keeps on going until it reaches the dentin. At this point, you might feel some pain in your tooth. If the acid eats all the way through to the pulp, where the nerves live, then you'll definitely feel pain. You have a toothache.

This tooth is covered in cavity-causing plaque.

A dentist uses a drill to clear out a cavity in a tooth.

Like most problems, cavities are easier to fix the earlier you catch them. Dentists look for cavities when they are cleaning your teeth. Dentists can spot cavities by the telltale brown, soft spots they leave on your teeth. These are the spots where your teeth are rotting away.

GROSS FACT #9

Your mouth isn't the only source of tooth-attacking acid. Your stomach makes about 4 pints (1.9 liters) of acid every day. Your stomach squirts the acid all over food as it digests. Usually, this acid stays safely in your stomach. But when you vomit, you can imagine what happens. Yep! All that acid comes up your throat and into your mouth. When people vomit a lot, their teeth begin to rot from all the acid. Gross!

EXPERIMENT: HOW ACID WORKS

Here's a simple way to see how tooth acid eats away at your teeth. You'll need a hard-boiled egg, a bowl, and some vinegar. Then follow these simple steps.

1) Pour the vinegar into the bowl.
2) Let the egg sit in the bowl of vinegar for about a day.
3) Examine the egg to see if the vinegar has eaten away at the shell.

Vinegar is an acid—similar to the one made by the bacteria living in your mouth. The vinegar eats away at the egg's shell in the same way mouth acid eats away at your tooth enamel. The longer the shell is exposed to acid, the more it will break down.

To stop cavities from rotting any more of your teeth, dentists put in fillings. First, the dentist scrapes out the rot and the area around the rot to make sure no little bits of food or bacteria are stuck in there. Then she fills in the hole with a filling—usually a soft metal.

After drilling, a dentist adds a filling so you don't have a big hole in your tooth.

ERUPTION!

CANKER SORES, COLD SORES, AND OTHER PROBLEMS

You know the feeling. You take a big gulp of orange juice one morning, and suddenly you're wincing in pain. Ouch! Who put burning acid in your OJ?

Of course, nothing has happened to your orange juice. It's your mouth. It's got a small volcano growing in it. OK—technically it's a canker sore, not a volcano. But either way, it's not much fun.

Canker sores are small, round sores that grow inside your mouth. They sprout up most often inside your cheeks, inside your lips, and on your tongue. You might start to feel a little tingle inside your mouth one day. By the next day, you might have a small, red bump. This probably won't hurt. But before long, that bump will explode. You've got a full-blown canker sore. It will turn into an open, festering sore, usually yellow or white in color. Surrounding that is a border of red, irritated skin. Then, just before they begin to heal, the sores often turn a grimy shade of gray. Canker sores are usually about a quarter of an inch (6 millimeters) in diameter.

GROSS FACT #10

Some people get canker sores that are 1 inch (25 mm) wide! And if they're really bad, they might rupture and bleed. Nasty!

Canker sores usually take one to two weeks to heal.

OW! THEY HURT TOO!

Usually the intense pain lasts for two to three days. Then there's often milder pain for up to a week. It may take two to three weeks for the sore to heal completely.

You'll notice the pain most when you eat or drink something that's spicy, salty, or acidic. Acidic foods are ones that have a high acid content, like oranges, grapefruits, and vinegar. Sometimes when you have a canker sore, you'll want to avoid those foods for a few days. You'll also want to be careful when you're brushing your teeth. If you've never experienced the feeling of jamming a toothbrush into an open canker sore, consider yourself lucky!

If you've got a canker sore, be careful with citrus fruits.

WHAT CAUSES THOSE LITTLE VOLCANOES?

If you've ever had a canker sore, then you probably have one question: how can I never get one again? Unfortunately, there's no sure way to avoid canker sores. Scientists aren't even entirely sure what causes them. Some think it has something to do with the body's immune system. The immune system is the body's first line of defense against invading viruses, bacteria, and other enemies. When your mouth gets a small injury, the immune system might kick into high gear and attack. The end result is—you guessed it!—a painful, pulsing, open canker sore.

TIP: CHECK YOUR TOOTHPASTE

Some scientists believe that people are more likely to get repeat canker sores when they use toothpaste with the ingredient sodium lauryl sulfate in it. They think that this drying ingredient may weaken the skin and make it easier for canker sores to develop.

GROSS FACT #11

Salt and canker sores don't get along very well. Don't believe it? When you've got a canker sore, rub a few grains of salt into it. (On second thought, why don't you just take my word for it? It's a brand of pain you'll be better off just imagining.)

Canker sores could also be allergic reactions to foods. Or they may form when a person is under a lot of stress. Some doctors think a lack of vitamin B or the mineral iron may cause canker sores.

Scientists do know a few things about canker sores for sure. They show up most often in people between the ages of ten and forty. They also seem to run in families. So if your parents got lots of canker sores, chances are that you will too.

SAY WHAT?
Aphthous ulcer is the scientific name for canker sore.

AHH! GET YOUR COLD SORES AWAY FROM ME!

A KISSING DISEASE?

What?! Can you really get a disease from kissing?!?

Yes, it's true! If you kiss someone on the lips, you can get a nasty flare-up right where the smooch happened. A big, festering red blob right on your lips? Ack! It's a cold sore!

OK. Cold sores aren't exactly caused by kissing. But kissing—or sharing a glass, straw, spoon, or...well, you get the idea—can spread the virus that causes these outbreaks. You might have heard them called by their nickname: fever blisters. Or maybe you've heard their full name: herpes simplex. Sounds scary, right? Don't worry too much. Cold sores are annoying, but they're not really dangerous.

Here's a close-up of the herpes simplex virus, which causes cold sores.

Cold sores usually start with a little tingling in one spot. Within a day or two, nasty little blisters filled with a sticky yellow fluid pop up. And it gets worse from there. Soon the blisters pop. That yellow goo inside oozes out. The goo then hardens into a sick-looking yellow crust. After about a week, the crust flakes away. Whew!

Lots of people carry the cold sore virus. And once you have it, you can't get rid of it. But you can live with it pretty easily. And you can follow some tips to try not to spread it.

1. **No kissing—ever.** (Just kidding. You actually can kiss without spreading cold sores—as long as you don't have any open sores.)
2. **No eating—ever.** (Yep, just kidding again. Just try not to share glasses, straws, forks, etc.)
3. **No sharing makeup, lip balm, or toothbrushes—ever.** (Not kidding about this one.)

Pucker up! Here's a mouth infested by cold sores.

Check out this close-up of leukoplakia.

OTHER ERUPTIONS

By now you're probably thinking: *EWW!* Canker sores and cold sores! Could it get any worse? Funny you should ask.

Some serious diseases, like chicken pox or the measles, can settle in around the mouth. Usually they announce their presence as red spots or rashes. Luckily, they go away when you get rid of the viruses that cause these diseases.

Leukoplakia is even grosser. It's a whitish rash that creeps inside some people's cheeks. Most times, only smokers get leukoplakia. But sometimes, people who have a habit of chewing on the inside of their cheeks can develop this dangerous rash.

CANDIDIASIS

GROSS FACT #12

If a doctor tells you that you have candidiasis, look out! It may sound like candy, but it means "mouth fungus." *YUCK!*

Some eruptions happen at the very back of your mouth, in your tonsils. As tonsils shed dead cells, some people end up with little white hills of dead cells on their tonsils. These are called tonsil stones. If they get big enough, they can flake off into the back of your throat. If you ever find yourself swallowing something soft and chunky and don't know where it came from, a tonsil stone is a good bet. They're harmless, but they taste terrible.

The bottom line is: your mouth is a twenty-four-hour-a-day saliva pool for millions of strange little critters. They even get buffet service every time you eat. So it's no surprise that some strange things happen in and around your mouth. There's no telling what might happen if you don't keep them under control!

GLOSSARY

acid: a sour-tasting substance. Acid made by bacteria in your mouth can eat away at your teeth.

amoeba: a microscopic, one-celled creature that lives inside your mouth and helps to kill bacteria

bacteria: microscopic living things that exist all around and inside you

canker sore: a small, round sore that grows inside your mouth

cavity: a hole in a tooth caused by decay

cold sore: a mouth ulcer caused by the herpes simplex virus

dentin: a hard yellow material in the center of teeth

digest: to break down food so it can be used for energy

enamel: the hard outer coating of the tooth

enzyme: a protein that causes chemical reactions to occur in the body. One kind of enzyme helps in digestion.

hydrogen sulfur: a foul-smelling chemical that is released by bacteria in the mouth

immune system: the system that protects the body against disease and infection

leukoplakia: a condition in which irritation causes thick white patches to form inside the mouth

lysozyme: a kind of protein found in saliva and tears

mucus: a slimy fluid that coats and protects the inside of your mouth, nose, throat, and other breathing passages

nerve: a thin fiber that sends messages back and forth between your brain and the rest of the body

plaque: a mixture of leftover food, bacteria, and other substances that forms on teeth, especially between teeth and at the edge of the gums

pulp: the soft center of the tooth. The pulp contains nerves and blood vessels.

saliva: clear liquid in your mouth that keeps it moist and helps you swallow and begin to digest food

salivary amylase: an enzyme in saliva that begins digestion by breaking down starches in the mouth

salivary glands: small groups of cells that make and release saliva into the mouth. The three main pairs are the parotid glands, the submandibular glands, and the sublingual glands.

tartar: plaque that has hardened on the tooth

virus: a microscopic living organism that causes disease

SELECTED BIBLIOGRAPHY

Bowen, Richard. "Pathology of the Digestive System." *Colorado State University*. July 5, 2006. http://www .vivo.colostate.edu/hbooks/pathphys/digestion/index .html (March 14, 2008).

Mayo Foundation for Medical Education and Research. "Canker Sore." *MayoClinic.com*. January 31, 2008. http://www.mayoclinic.com/health/canker-sore/ DS00354 (March 16, 2008).

Nemours Foundation. "Taking Care of Your Teeth." *KidsHealth*. 2008. http://www.kidshealth.org/teen/ your_body/take_care/teeth.html (March 14, 2008).

———. "What's Spit?" *KidsHealth*. 2008. http://www .kidshealth.org/kid/talk/yucky/spit.html (March 14, 2008).

Rauch, Daniel. "Canker Sores." *MedlinePlus*. December 18, 2006. http://www.nlm.nih.gov/medlineplus/ency/ article/000998.htm (March 14, 2008).

Silverstein, Alvin, Virginia Silverstein, and Laura Silverstein Nunn. *Tooth Decay and Cavities*. My Health series. Danbury, CT: Grolier Publishing, 1999.

FURTHER READING

Cobb, Vicki. *Your Body Battles a Cavity*. Minneapolis: Millbrook Press, 2009. Read about the battle that happens in your mouth when saliva fights the acid and bacteria trying to destroy your teeth. Cartoon illustrations and colorful photomicrographs help bring this battle to life.

Gower, Timothy. *This Book Bites!: Or, Why Your Mouth Is More Than Just a Hole in Your Head*. Reading, MA: Planet Dexter, 1999. Find out more about your mouth in this book that includes the answers to questions such as "Why does my voice sound dorky on tape?" and "Why do some people eat dirt?"

Haggis-On-Whey, Doris, and Benny Haggis-On-Whey. *Your Disgusting Head: The Darkest, Most Offensive and Moist Secrets of Your Ears, Mouth and Nose*. New York: Simon & Schuster, 2004. This hilarious book is filled with utterly disgusting true and not-so-true facts about the human head.

Kachlany, Scott C. *Infectious Diseases of the Mouth*. Deadly Diseases and Epidemics series. New York: Chelsea House Publications, 2007. Discover the science behind all sorts of mouth-related infections.

Masoff, Joy. *Oh, Yuck! The Encyclopedia of Everything Nasty*. New York: Workman Publishing Company, 2000. This book presents a huge collection of gross, putrid, stomach-turning facts.

Stangl, Jean. *What Makes You Cough, Sneeze, Burp, Hiccup, Blink, Yawn, Sweat, and Shiver?* London: Franklin Watts, 2000. Read all about these bodily phenomena in this fact-filled book.

Taking Care of Your Teeth
http://www.kidshealth.org/kid/stay_healthy/body/teeth.html
Get kid-friendly information about how to keep your teeth healthy.

Viegas, Jennifer. *The Mouth and Nose: Learning How We Taste and Smell*. 3-D Library of the Human Body series. New York: Rosen Publishing, 2001. Learn more about how your mouth helps out in tasting and smelling.

Weiner, Esther. *The Incredible Human Body*. New York: Scholastic, 1999. This reference book is packed with information and activities to help you explore the rest of the human body.

INDEX

About the Author

Sandy Donovan has written many books for young readers. She lives in Minneapolis and is an expert on farting and belching thanks to her sons, Henry and Gus.

About the Illustrator

Michael Slack's illustrations have appeared in books, magazines, advertisements, and on TV. His paintings and drawings have been exhibited in the United States and Europe. Michael lives in the San Francisco Bay area.

Photo Acknowledgments

The images in this book are used with the permission of: © Dr. Dennis Kunkel Microscopy, Inc. /Visuals Unlimited, Inc., pp. 1(background), 3 (background), 24 (top), 37 (bottom); © Dr Gladden Willis/Visuals Unlimited, Inc., p. 4; © Plush Studios/Digital Vision/Getty Images, p. 5; © Todd Strand/Independent Picture Service, pp. 6 (bottom), 31 (top); © Biodisc/Visuals Unlimited, Inc., p. 7; © Dr. Alvin Telser/ Visuals Unlimited, Inc., p. 8 (bottom left); Custom Medical Stock Photo, pp. 9, 23(smile); Reflexstock /© Radius Images, p. 10 (top); © Dr. Richard Kessel & Dr. Randy Kardon/Tissues & Organs/Visuals Unlimited, Inc., p. 11; © David Trood/The Image Bank/Getty Images, p. 12; © Dr. Dennis Kunkel/PHOTOTAKE, p. 14; © Image Source/Getty Images, p. 15; © Alex Balako/Shuterstock Images, p. 16; © Thierry Berrod, Mona Lisa Production/Science Photo Library/Photo Researchers, Inc., p. 17; © Manfred Kage/Peter Arnold Inc., p. 18; © Dr Stanley Flegler/Getty Images, p. 19; © SCIMAT/Science Photo Library/Photo Researchers, Inc., p. 21 (top); © BananaStock/ SuperStock, p. 21; © Adamr/Dreamstime.com, p. 23 (teeth); © Homestudiofoto/Dreamstime. com, p. 23 (magnifying glass); © BSIP/Benedet/ PHOTOTAKE, p. 24 (bottom); © Educational Images, Ltd./Custom Medical Stock Photo, p. 25; © BSIP/ PHOTOTAKE, p. 26; © Steve Gschmeissner/ Science Photo Library/Photo Researchers, Inc., p. 27 (bottom); Courtesy of the National Museum of Dentistry, Baltimore, MD. p. 27 (top); © iStockphoto.com/Eric Delmer, p. 28 (top); © David MacCarthy/Science Photo Library/Photo Researchers, Inc., p. 29 (bottom); © Medicimage /Visuals Unlimited, Inc., p. 30; Edward H. Gill/Custom Medical Stock Photo, pp. 31 (bottom), 34 (top); © Edward Kinsman/Photo Researchers, Inc., p. 33 (top); © ISM/PHOTOTAKE, p. 33; © Anna Sedneva/Shuterstock Images, p. 34 (bottom); © Dr. Gopal Murti/Visuals Unlimited, Inc., p. 35 (top); © Stockphoto.com/Bogdan Dumitru, p. 35 (bottom); © Science Photo Library/Photo Researchers, Inc., p. 38; © NMSB/Custom Medical Stock Photo, p. 39; © Scientifica/Visuals Unlimited, Inc., p. 40 (top).

Front cover: Reflexstock/ © Radius Images, (big mouth); © Luminis/Dreamstime.com (toothbrush), © iStockphoto.com/Sharon Dominick (woman making silly face); © JL Carson/ Custom Medical Stock Photo (background micrograph).